Just My

On Friday, Ben couldn't wait for school to finish. He was looking forward to the long weekend.

On Saturday morning,
his dad took him to buy
some Reeboks.

They looked and looked, but
there weren't any in Ben's size.
"Just my luck!" said Ben.

On Saturday afternoon, his brother took him to Luna Park.

They went straight to Ben's
favourite ride, but it was closed.
"Just my luck!" said Ben.

On Sunday Ben took his skateboard to Kate's place. "Let's go and try out the new bowl," said Kate.

But all the big kids had got there first.

"Just my luck!" said Ben.

On Sunday night, Sam came to sleep at Ben's house.

They were having great fun,
but then Sam got homesick and
his mum had to come and get him.
"Just my luck!" said Ben.

On Monday morning, Ben set up a stall outside his house.

Fresh Orange Juice

He had lots of customers,
but then a dog knocked over the
table.
"Just my luck!" said Ben.

"Cheer up," said Ben's mum.
"Tonight I'm making your
favourite roast dinner."
"Yum," said Ben.

But in the afternoon the power went off – and she couldn't use the stove. They had to get take-aways instead.